O HOLY COW!

The Selected Verse of
Phil Rizzuto

O HOLY COW!

The Selected Verse of
Phil Rizzuto

Edited by
Tom Peyer and Hart Seely

With an introduction by
Roy Blount, Jr.

THE ECCO PRESS

To my brother Pete and his son Bob,
two of baseball's mightiest.—T. P.

To my sons, Hart and Kyle.—H. S.

Grateful acknowledgment is made to the New York
Yankees and WPIX-TV for their assistance in making this
book possible. And, of course, to Dallas Crow.

Copyright © 1993 by Phil Rizzuto
All rights reserved

The Ecco Press
100 West Broad Street
Hopewell, NJ 08525
Published simultaneously in Canada by
Penguin Books Canada Ltd., Ontario
Printed in the United States of America
Designed by Debby Jay
First Edition

Library of Congress Cataloging-in-Publication Data

Rizzuto, Phil, 1918–
    O holy cow!: the selected verse of Phil Rizzuto / edited by
  Hart Seely and Tom Peyer.—1st ed.
      p.   cm.
    $8.95
    1. New York Yankees (Baseball team)—Poetry.
  2. Baseball—Poetry.
  I. Seely, Hart, 1952–   . II. Peyer, Tom, 1954–   . III. Title.
  PS3568.I86015   1993
  811'.54—dc20   92-40352 CIP
    ISBN 0-88001-325-7 (paper)

The text of this book is set in Century Schoolbook.

Contents

Acknowledgments

We tell ya.
We'd like to thank
The following folks
For their wisdom,
And spiritual guidance
And whatever:
There's Jeff Z. Klein,
And Frank Deford,
And Tom Riker,
And Janice Whitcraft,
And Susan Tuohy,
And WPIX-TV,
And *The Village Voice,*
And The New York Yankees,
And The Miley Collection,
And Danrick Enterprises,
And Cora.
Unbelievable.

Hart Seely and Tom Peyer

Introduction to the Rizzuto Poems

Roy Blount, Jr.

> If the Scooter ever makes it
> To the Baseball Hall of Fame,
> As I believe he should,
> My own closest brush with diamond
> Immortality will be
> The flu he had once
> When I interviewed him.
> He got it "from that Coleman,"
> He said, meaning the old Yankee
> Second-sacker Gerry.
> And then
> I came down with it.
> Score that 4 to 6 to me—
> One of my greatest sports thrills.
>
> As to whether my verse is catching
> Any quality of his,

note that I am throwing up my hands now and sliding into prose. Certainly my lines on how he gave me the flu are not in the same league as his on how he gave Yogi Berra squirrels, ("Squirrels.")[1] Mine on getting a bug, to put it another way, lack both the quickness and the range of the Scooter's on getting butterflies, ("Field of Butterflies.")

How does he do it? You can't steal first base, baseball people say, but Rizzuto obviates the intentional fallacy. Less self-consciously even than a Homer,[2] he broadcasts his poetry orally and leaves the writing-down to less imma-

---

[1]When Berra and he were roommates, the Scooter told me in another interview, he would get Yogi to sleep by reading him bedtime stories.

[2]One definition of a homer is a sports commentator who shamelessly favors the home team.

nent[3] sensibilities. The Scooter's lyricism springs not from any imperative to advance literary tradition but from a half century of familiarity with baseball's various means of transmission: for instance, wood. In "DiMaggio's Bat"[4] Rizzuto conveys DiMaggio's understanding of wood:

> *Being an old fisherman*
> *He knew about the trees.*

What I just did there was hop and scramble into position to quote one of my favorite Rizzuto passages, and did I ever do it awkwardly. Whereas Rizzuto can go from Dickie Thon to Puerto Rico to World War II to Velarde to Stankiewicz ("Dickie Poem Number One") with an easy rhythm. Well, not *easy*. Let me try to put it this way:

> They called him Scooter
> For his movement on the field,
> Picking up grounders
> And laying down bunts
> And running them out.
> And so does his mind scoot,
> As did that of
> William Carlos Williams,
> Who wrote:

> > *. . . you have it over a troop*
> > *of artists—*
> > *unless one should scour the world—*
> > *you have the ground sense necessary.*

> Scooter had the ground sense,
> All right,
> And it transferred to the booth,
> And it took to the air,
> And it fascinates millions;

---

[3]Is that not exactly the word I have in mind? To quote the Scooter himself: *No?/ No kiddin'?/ Great.*

[4]No homer jokes here.

And now here it is
Looking good on paper.
What boots it that we scour the world
Or at least the left side
Of the infield
For artistry any further?

    Great poet.

(As the Scooter himself says
Of Walden.)

    Great great poet.

O HOLY COW!

The Selected Verse of
Phil Rizzuto

Field of Butterflies

Absolutely!
If you don't get a little,
A few butterflies,
No matter what you do,
On the first day of anything,
You're not human.

April 12, 1991
New York at Kansas City
Storm Davis pitching to Steve Sax
First inning, no outs, bases empty
(First batter, opening day)
No score

Alienation

I think my head shrinks a little
In this indoor stadium.

I am . . .

The mike is getting bigger.
And I have to tighten it.

May 2, 1987
New York at Minnesota
Tommy John pitching to Al Newman
Third inning, two outs, two base runners
Yankees lead 3–2

To Be Alone

Hey White
You know where your loyalties are?

Right here.
The old pinstripes.

No.

You never wore them.
So you have a right to sing the blues.

May 12, 1987
New York at Chicago
Bill Long pitching to Dan Pasqua
Second inning, no outs, bases empty
White Sox lead 1–0

On the Couch
with Myself

I wonder if they work
Like the regular psychologists
And psychiatrists
Where you do all the talking
And they just listen
And nod.

April 12, 1991
New York at Kansas City
Mark Davis pitching to Steve Sax
Ninth inning, two outs, bases empty
Royals lead 9–5

Chaos

This is very interesting.
Forget the game.
Right here.
Here's a guy can't see.
All right,
Gene Larkin is the NO!
Gene Larkin?
What did he do?
Base on balls.

June 22, 1991
Minnesota at New York
Wade Taylor pitching to Shane Mack
Sixth inning, two outs, one base runner
Twins lead 2–0

Time and Money

Oh! TIME! No! TIME!
Puckett had asked for time!
Puckett had asked for time!
And the plate umpire was on the ball.

Remember the time that cost Don Money
   A grand-slam home run in Milwaukee?

See him there.
He's holding the hand.
That's when he asked for it.
And everybody watching,
The pitcher and the runner,
Didn't see him call . . .
Time!

May 8, 1987, WPIX-TV
New York at Minnesota
Dennis Rasmussen pitching to Kirby Puckett
A pick-off attempt at second base
Top of the first, one out, no count, no score
Final: Twins 2, Yankees 0

6

My Secret

When I'm driving
To Yankee Stadium and back,
I do it so often.

I don't remember passing lights.
I don't remember paying tolls
Coming over the bridge.

Going back over the bridge,
I remember . . .

August 19, 1992
Oakland at New York
Mike Moore pitching to Mel Hall
Fifth inning, one out, bases empty
Yankees lead 4–1

7

From Slumber I Heard
the Men at Work

I.

Friday,
When I was forced
To leave the game after six innings,
You know,
I almost came back in the 13th inning,
Moore.
I want you to know I was thinking
Of Murcer and Seaver there.

II.

I woke up,
And it was like,
Like a nightmare.
I said,
"Could the game still be going on?"
And sure enough.
I started to get dressed.
And then the 14th inning came.
If it had gone another inning,
I'd have been there.

> August 30, 1992
> New York at Minnesota
> Russ Springer pitching to Chili Davis
> Sixth inning, two outs, bases empty
> Twins lead 5–1

Hero or the Goat

All right this is it,
The whole season coming down
To just one ball game,
And every mistake will be magnified,
And every great play will be magnified,
And it's a tough night for the players,
I'll tell ya.
I know last night,
Being in the same situation many times
With the great Yankee teams of the past,
You stay awake,
And you dream,
And you think of what might be,
If you are the hero or the goat.

October 14, 1976
AMERICAN LEAGUE EAST PLAYOFF
Final game
Kansas City at New York
Pregame show

9

Imagine

One ball two strikes on Nettles,
Every pitch and every play
So important in this ball game.
Imagine two teams
Coming down to the end of the season,
Both winning 99 games,
Everybody thought 95 would win the pennant.
And it all boils down
To this one playoff game.
All right, Torrez ready.
The one-two pitch . . .

October 2, 1978
AMERICAN LEAGUE EAST PLAYOFF
New York at Boston
Mike Torrez pitching to Graig Nettles
(He pops up to shortstop.)
Fourth inning, one out, one base runner
Red Sox lead 1–0

Telly, Cary, and Frank

All right,
A big hubbub right in back of the Yankee dugout,
Dead center,
Telly Savalas!
We might have to ask him to put a hat on his head,
It's shining up here,
Some glare,
But that's the thing lately,
They say being bald is very sexy,
All right,
I tell ya,
Just about everybody you want to name
Will be here tonight.
Cary Grant hasn't missed a game
Here at Yankee Stadium at the playoffs.
Frank Sinatra has been here.
And we're ready.

October 14, 1976
AMERICAN LEAGUE EAST PLAYOFF
Final game
Kansas City at New York
Ed Figueroa pitching to Al Cowens
First inning, no outs, bases empty
No score

They Own the Wind

i tell ya,
did you take notice of the flag?
i couldn't believe it.
just as jim rice came to the plate,
the wind started blowing to left field.
it not only helped yastrzemski's homer,
but it hurt jackson's,
the wind was blowing to right field
when jackson hit the fly ball,
when yaz hit the homer
the wind was blowing to left field,
kept it from going foul.
strike one to piniella.
somebody told me
the red sox control the elements up here
i didn't believe 'em until today

October 2, 1978
AMERICAN LEAGUE EAST PLAYOFF
New York at Boston
Mike Torrez pitching to Lou Piniella
Fourth inning, no outs, bases empty
Red Sox lead 1–0

Prayer for the Captain

There's a little prayer I always say
Whenever I think of my family or when I'm flying,
When I'm afraid, and I am afraid of flying.
It's just a little one. You can say it no matter what,
Whether you're Catholic or Jewish or Protestant or
        whatever.
And I've probably said it a thousand times
Since I heard the news on Thurman Munson.

It's not trying to be maudlin or anything.
His Eminence, Cardinal Cooke, is going to come out
And say a little prayer for Thurman Munson.
But this is just a little one I say time and time again,
It's just: *Angel of God, Thurman's guardian dear,*
To whom his love commits him here there or everywhere,
Ever this night and day be at his side,
To light and guard, to rule and guide.

For some reason it makes me feel like I'm talking to
        Thurman,
Or whoever's name you put in there,
Whether it be my wife or any of my children, my parents
        or anything.
It's just something to keep you really from going bananas.
Because if you let this,
If you keep thinking about what happened, and you can't
        understand it,
That's what really drives you to despair.

Faith. You gotta have faith.
You know, they say time heals all wounds,
And I don't quite agree with that a hundred percent.

It gets you to cope with wounds.
You carry them the rest of your life.

August 3, 1979
Baltimore at New York
Pregame show

14

The Man in the Moon

The Yankees have had a traumatic four days.
Actually five days.
That terrible crash with Thurman Munson.
To go through all that agony,
And then today,
You and I along with the rest of the team
Flew to Canton for the services,
And the family . . .
    Very upset.

You know, it might,
It might sound a little corny.
But we have the most beautiful full moon tonight.
And the crowd,
Enjoying whatever is going on right now.
They say it might sound corny,
But to me it's some kind of a,
    Like an omen.

Both the moon and Thurman Munson,
Both ascending up into heaven.
I just can't get it out of my mind.
I just saw that full moon,
And it just reminded me of Thurman.
    And that's it.

> August 6, 1979
> Baltimore at New York
> Ron Guidry pitching to Lee May
> Fifth inning, bases empty, no outs
> Orioles lead 1–0

The Bridge

Two balls and a strike.
You know what they had on TV today, White?
Bridge on the River Kwai.
Everybody should have gotten an Academy Award for
    that movie.
I don't know how many times I've seen it.
About forty times.
Alec Guinness!
William Holden!
Three and one the count.
I just heard somebody whistle.
You know that song?
That's what they whistle.
Nobody out.
And he pops it up.

May 5, 1987
New York at Chicago
Joe Niekro pitching to Carlton Fisk
Second inning, no outs, bases empty
No score

Poem for *The Last Picture Show*

Wait a minute, that's right!
He's from this little town.
And the cars, he said.
They ride up and down on Main Street all night.
And they never get out of their cars.
And that's the way it was in that movie.
With those old model, old . . .
O, that was really really an excellent picture.

> July 29, 1991
> Oakland at New York
> Jeff Johnson pitching to Willie Wilson
> First inning, one out, bases empty
> No score

Never Say Never

Never!
That—
NEVER!
I shouldn't say "Never."
Even James Bond said
"Never say never."
That was a hit.
Right?

> June 27, 1991
> New York at Boston
> Tom Bolton pitching to Randy Velarde
> Third inning, two outs, one base runner
> Yankees lead 4–0

Vincent

O wait a minute.
You gotta take one shot of this.
'Cause this is a true . . .
This is,
This is true.
I was,
Say . . .
That?
HEY THAT'S VINCENT GARDENIA!
HEY!
O he was in *Death Wish*.
With Charles Bronson.
He was mean.
And he really got shot up.
Holy cow.

August 9, 1992
Boston at New York
Sam Militello pitching to Jack Clark
Second inning, no outs, bases empty
Yankees lead 3–0

19

I Never Cried

You know where that came from?
That saying?
Murcer?
That movie,
A League of Their Own.
With the gals.
Tom Hanks is a manager.
And he's a riot.
He's drunk all the time
At the beginning.
And then he turns out to,
One girl cries,
Because she didn't get a hit
Or something.
And he screams,
"There's no crying in baseball."

August 15, 1992
New York at Chicago
Charlie Hough pitching to Bernie Williams
Third inning, one out, bases empty
No score

I Walk with Fear

Boy
I never forget
The first Dracula movie
I ever saw.
BELA LUGOSI!

June 27, 1991
New York at Boston
Tom Bolton pitching to Roberto Kelly
Third inning, no outs, bases empty
Yankees lead 2–0

21

The Question of White's Whereabouts

That was a weird play!
Wait a minute!
That hit the bat twice!
That should be a foul ball!
Here comes Piniella out!
That hit the bat twice!
Now he's saying he's off the bag!
Son of a gun!
I can't believe that!
Let's look at this!
Look at that!
That ball came up and hit the bat!
Twice!
White, where were you when we needed you?

May 2, 1987
Minnesota at New York
Juan Berenguer pitching to Willie Randolph
(Ground ball to the pitcher)
Seventh inning, two outs, bases empty
Yankees lead 5–2

White's Secret

You know what I did?
I forgot
I don't like your lineup card, White.
I like mine better.
But unfortunately
I left mine at home.
I did not bring today's lineup card.

So I borrowed one from Bill White.
He's the professional type.
You know, Martin?
He's got all . . .
I can't figure half the stuff on this card.
Why you need it.
But he does his homework.
He does it well.

But anyway,
Oh yeah.
He's got the highlights.
He's on the ball.
But where Kunkel's name is ninth,
I put the strikeout by Brower.
Oh, he jammed him.
Foul back.
What happened?

May 13, 1987
New York at Texas
Dennis Rasmussen pitching to Bob Brower
Third inning, two out, bases empty
Yankees lead 3–0

Forever Young

Bobby Thigpen out there.
Number thirty-seven.
That's the guy in the Peanuts cartoon.
Pigpen.
That's a joke.
That guy in Peanuts with Charlie Brown.
He's always dirty.
Oh yeah.
Every day.
Orphan Annie.
You know,
She hasn't aged in thirty-two years.

May 12, 1987
Chicago at New York
Bill Long pitching to Don Mattingly
Sixth inning, no outs, one base runner
Yankees lead 3–1

The Penguin

O THAT'S GONE!
HOLY COW!
WATCH THE—
Look at the Penguin!
It's not gone.

I was watching him run.
Wait a minute.
When he hit it
That was the funniest run I've ever seen.
Watch this.

> May 31, 1987
> Oakland at New York
> Tommy John pitching to Ron Cey
> Second inning, no outs, bases empty
> (Long fly to left)
> Tie score 1–1

25

T-Bone

One ball, one strike
Two out, two on
The Yankees trail four to one
In the bottom of the seventh.
Michelle wants to say
"Happy birthday to T-Bone."
That's his name: T-Bone.
The runners leading away . . .

July 26, 1991
California at New York
Mark Langston pitching to Bernie Williams
Game status as indicated

26

To Speak with Espy,
to Smile with Tears

I just told him, I said:
"Look,
You're a professional.
You've got to stop this squabbling in the papers.
It's the worst thing you can do.
Just go out there and play your regular game.
Show them that you're capable
Of playing every day."
He smiled for the first time.
I said, "Geh."
(Now you won't believe this.)
I said, "GET THREE FOR THREE!"
I know . . .
It sounds like I made it up.
I really did make it up.
It's such a lousy game
That I gotta make up something.

April 12, 1991
New York at Kansas City
Storm Davis pitching to Steve Sax
Seventh inning, no outs, one base runner
(Following Alvaro Espinoza's third hit)
Royals lead 8–4

27

The Way Mattingly
Wants Them to Do

Down in Florida, I'm telling you
They're rooting so hard,
They count, they say:
"We gotta win some games!"
And to see something like this,
You know, with the fans,
The ballplayers getting excited
The way Mattingly wants them to do,
Instead of laying back
And waiting to get beat,
The way so many ball clubs used to do
Against the Yankees,
You know, they used to say,
"Some way they're going to beat us."
And they do.

May 10, 1991
Oakland at New York
Greg Cadaret pitching to Willie Wilson
Eighth inning, no outs, bases empty
Yankees lead 5–3

Challenge to Youth

I tell you what I would change:
That NO BALK to second base.
You know,
You can do anything to second base.
Yeah, I never did like that.
What would you change?

May 10, 1991
Oakland at New York
John Habyan pitching to Mark McGwire
Seventh inning, one out, one base runner
Orioles lead 3–2

Champion

Remember that fellow I told you.
Champ Marble?
Champ Marble.
He's a hundred and two years old.
When he was a hundred years old I told you.
Last year he was a hundred and one.
This year he is a hundred and two.
Played golf with him over at Upper Montclair Country
      Club.
He's probably in bed now.
A little low.
One ball, two strikes.
His name is Champ Marble.
James F. Marble to be exact.
I mean really a tremendous man.
He doesn't wear glasses.
No hearing aid.
Sees better than me.
Hits better than me.
Better than me.
High and tight.
Two and two.

April 12, 1991
New York at Kansas City
Chuck Cary pitching to Gary Thurman
Third inning, two outs, two base runners
Score tied 3–3

Giliad

I was with Gil McDougald the other day.
Oh boy.
He looks great.
Playing golf over in Spring Lake's Golf Club.
Sad thing is that,
You know,
He's totally deaf now.
FOUL! He stays alive!
Still got a great sense of humor.
But he had to retire,
Because he was getting all those phone calls
In his business.
And he just couldn't,
No way could he hear anything.
So he sold his business.
Very happy.
They love him down there at Spring Lake.

But I was very happy.
'Cause he does talk and tell stories and,
He's not a good listener,
But one thing he told me
That I was very happy about—
LOW! BALL FOUR!
WHAT AN EYE BY NOKES!
How do you like that?
Behind 0 and 2 and he works his way for a walk!
You know what McDougald told me when he saw me?
He hadn't seen me for a while.
He said, "I wanna tell you something.
You're not as ugly as you look on TV."

He said to me.
I said, "Thanks Gil."

May 25, 1991
New York at Baltimore
Mike Flanagan pitching to Matt Nokes
Ninth inning, no outs, bases empty
Score tied 4–4

Kubek and Trautwig and
Phillips or Powers

Tony is having a little problem
With his uh—oh yeah, Traut,
I want to tell you something about Trautwig.
He had the greatest interview that I have ever heard.
With Richie Phillips the basketball umpire.
Referee.
I gotta get him over here.
Holy.

Can I, uh, can we give . . .
Give him the microphone
Just to talk about this?

Look at Kubek over there.
Kubek's voice is going.
I might have to stick around
But Al Trautwig is here
And I heard an interview
I couldn't believe it
With Richie Phillips . . .
Richie Powers.
I just want to tell you
I just couldn't believe it.
Kubek over there.

I tell you.
I couldn't believe what I was hearing.
About Richie Powers
When he said to you,
"The last thing I think about before I go to sleep,
Is this the night I'm gonna commit suicide?"
Am I right?

I tell you,
This was really great.

August 11, 1991
Detroit at New York
Paul Gibson pitching to Pat Kelly
Sixth inning, no outs, bases empty
Yankees lead 8–6

Dickie Poem Number One

Dickie Thon the batter.
Now way way back when he first came
Into the big leagues,
I mention the fact that I used to play
With his grandfather.
Baseball.
Sandlot baseball.
He went away to the minor leagues.
And during the service time,
He was in Puerto Rico.
And he was a very
Astute young man.
Don't forget,
This was way back
In the Second World War.
Grounder to short,
And Velarde just flips
To Stankiewicz for the force.
And that'll do it.
And I'll finish my story later.

April 27, 1992
Texas at New York
Scott Sanderson pitching to Dickie Thon
Fourth inning, two outs, one base runner
Yankees lead 3–1

Dickie Poem Number Two

Wait!
I never finished
This story about Dickie Thon!
I told you I played ball
With his grandfather.
And,
And he was so on the ball.
When he went to Puerto Rico
He realized they didn't
Have washing machines.
Things we had in the States.
Ahhhhhhhhhhhh . . .
The son of a gun!
Hit the grounder.
I'll have to finish the story
Next home stand.
Three up.
Three down.

April 27, 1992
Texas at New York
Lee Guetterman pitching to Dickie Thon
Sixth inning, two outs, bases empty
Yankees lead 6–3

36

1961 and 1991

Oh man,
You talk about having fun broadcasting games.
That year, I mean, there were home runs every day.
There was nothing but a lot of runs.
Makes it a lot easier.
All right!
Here's Lovullo.
Torey Lovullo.
I've been calling him "Tony."
And he pops it up.

> April 13, 1991
> New York at Kansas City
> Bret Saberhagen pitching to Torey Lovullo
> Third inning, no outs, bases empty
> Royals lead 2–0

Remember When

O it was always intense.
Just as you said
And it was not a regular
Not a regular game at all.
It was every game meant so much,
You know,
One seemed to top the other.

May 28, 1991
Boston at New York
Roger Clemens pitching to Hensley Meulens
Fifth inning, no outs, bases empty
Red Sox lead 4–1

My Only Friend, the End

I.

And here comes Casey Stengel.
And I believe he's gonna call in the man
Who has been his insurance the last half of this season,
Louie Arroyo!
With the left-handed hitter up there,
Casey will probably bring in Arroyo,
And that's the sign he makes,
For the left-hander.
Terry is out of there.

II.

Louie Arroyo coming on,
Will be trying to get rid of Pete Runnels,
If he possibly can, .
And he's got himself a tough job,
As Jackie Jensen just told you,
Pete Runnels is the type hitter
Who does not worry
About whether it's a left-hander or right-hander
Out on the mound,
He as we all know can hit the ball
As hard to left field as he does to right field.
It's gonna be a battle now,
Pete just trying to meet the ball,
And Arroyo trying to outguess him on the hill.

III.

Pete Runnels the batter,
Runners at first and third,
The Yankees lead four to three,
We're in the bottom of the ninth inning,
Arroyo into the stretch position.

The pitch is POPPED FOUL
AND BOBBY RICHARDSON IS UNDER IT
AND MAKES THE CATCH,
AND THE YANKEES WIN THE PENNANT,
THE TWENTY-FIFTH PENNANT
IN THE YANKEES' CAREER.

September 25, 1960
Boston at New York
Luis Arroyo pitching to Pete Runnels
Ninth inning, two base runners, two out
Yankees lead 4–3

Poem No. 61

Here comes Roger Maris.
They're standing up.
Waiting to see if Roger
Is going to hit
Number sixty-one.
Here's the windup.
The pitch to Roger.
Way outside.
Ball one.

The fans are starting to boo.
Low . . .
Ball two.
That one was in the dirt.
And the boos get louder.
Two balls, no strikes
On Roger Maris . . .

Here's the windup.
Fastball
HIT DEEP TO RIGHT—
THIS COULD BE IT.
WAY BACK THERE.
HOLY COW.
   HE DID IT.
   SIXTY-ONE HOME RUNS.
They're fighting for the ball out there.

        October 1, 1961, WPIX-NY
        Boston at New York
        Roger Maris batting against Tracy Stallard
        Fourth inning, no score, bases empty
        Final: Yankees 1, Red Sox 0

A Life for Mickey

The pitch to Mick: a swing and a miss,
And, boy, he was going for the downs on that one.
Two balls, two strikes.
Sun shining brightly here today.
This is the best day we've had
Of the three days we've played ball here in Detroit.
All right, ready for the two-two delivery.
Wilson's pitch—is foul tipped,
And in and out of the glove of Freehan,
A life for Mickey.
And now Mick goes back,
Wants the pine tar rag, a little better grip.
Pepitone hands it to him. Two and two.
The scoreboard thought it was strike three.
Now they put the count up there again.
Two and two, one man out.
Earl Wilson ready to pitch to Mantle.
He kicks, delivers: it's high and outside,
Ball three, three and two,
Freehan gives the sign.
Wilson ready for the payoff pitch.
Here it is: And it's hit deep to right,
THAT'S GONE! WAY BACK UP THERE!
A two-run homer for Mantle,
Who has now homered in four consecutive ball games.
And suddenly it's a seven-to-four ball game.
Mickey Mantle really stroking that potato!

May 21, 1967
New York at Detroit
Earl Wilson pitching to Mickey Mantle
Seventh inning, one base runner, one out
Tigers lead 7–4

42

Confrontation

Ted Williams made this remark now.
And I'm not saying it
Because I agree with him wholeheartedly.
But he said,
"Pitchers are the dumbest ballplayers of all ballplayers.
Infielders, outfielders," he says.
" 'Cause all they know how to do is pitch.
And they only pitch one out of every five days."
Now I'm just saying,
What?
What did you think of that statement?
Bouncer.
And Sax to his left.
Throws him out.
One away.
I'm asking you a simple question, Seaver.
There he is.
He won't answer me.
How do you like my shirt?
You see my shirt?
Rocky Marciano.

July 23, 1991
Seattle at New York
Scott Kamieniecki pitching to Greg Briley
Seventh inning, no outs, bases empty
Mariners lead 2–1

DiMaggio's Bat

I started to tell you this story
And I was rudely interrupted by somebody.
Not Seaver though.
I want to make that clear . . .
Today,
When I went to get the newspaper
This gentleman,
His name is Phil,
Same as mine,
Brought in a bat.
I thought he was going to give it to me.
Joe DiMaggio's bat.
And it had "US ARMY" on it.
DiMag was in the army.
He got it in Hawaii.
His brother,
This Phil's brother,
Was stationed with DiMaggio.
And DiMaggio gave him a bat.
And you should see that thing.
And he wanted to know if it was worth money.
I said, "It's worth a lot of money.
And if we can get DiMaggio's name on it,
It'll be worth ten times more."
The wood . . .
I mean,
You couldn't chip that bat.
That's the way DiMaggio's wood was on the bats.
He would ask for that type of wood.

Being an old fisherman
He knew about the trees.

June 5, 1992
Detroit at New York
Scott Sanderson pitching to Lou Whitaker
Fourth inning, two outs, two base runners
Tigers lead 4–1

O What a Huddle Out There

I.

Now I had started to tell you
When I saw Billy Martin make the motion
For Gossage to come on
That it brings back some nightmares.
When George Brett in 1980,
The year the Royals beat the Yankees in the playoffs,
Right here at Yankee Stadium,
Hit a 95-mile-an-hour fastball thrown by the Gossage
A hundred twenty miles an hour into the upper deck
Here at Yankee Stadium.
And the best fastball pitcher in baseball
And just about the best fastball hitter in baseball,
George Brett,
What a confrontation.

The set, the pitch,
AND A DRIVE TO DEEP LEFT FIELD
And curving foul . . .
Holy cow.
Where's Bill White?
Bill White is in his car on the way home,
Not up here getting nervous and cold.
Long strike.

The set by Gossage, the pitch,
DEEP TO RIGHT FIELD
HOLY COW I DON'T BELIEVE IT!
HOME RUN FOR GEORGE BRETT!
I don't believe it,
That lightning could strike twice,
And Billy Martin now is coming out,
He wants to take a look at that bat,
But it's a little late.
I don't believe it.

I told you I have nightmares about this man.
Unbelievable!

Hey, they might have a point here!
Thurman Munson was called out after getting a base hit
Because there was pine tar above—
You can see the bat!
Well no you can't because we're not on TV,
Above the trademark!
And Billy Martin might have a valid point here!
That's the only way the Yankees can get out of this
        scrape.

Holy cow, I can't believe it.
Brett hit that ball nine miles.
Billy pointing to the bat!
Now, Thurman Munson had gotten a base hit out in
        Minnesota.
And the manager of the Twins at that time
Asked the umpire to look at the bat,
And they called Thurman Munson out,
And Martin has a very valid argument here.
And if he wins this,
There will be chaos.

Look at George Brett.
He's getting congratulated.
But there's a big huddle out there.
And the umpires, they've got to talk,
To get a calibrating machine out here
And calibrate this thing
And see just how high the pine tar is,
And there is a definite rule in the rule book
That you cannot have it above a certain distance!

O what a huddle out there.
They're really . . .
Billy Martin standing with his arms folded out there.
Boy, he was quickly off that bench.

WELL, LOOK WHO HAS RETURNED!
He made a U-turn on the bridge!
BILL WHITE IS BACK!
And they are about to make a decision
And this could be a momentous decision.
I can't tell by the way they're walking
Who's going to win this argument.

HE'S OUT!

II.

Well, I tell ya,
There's a rule,
A definite rule in the rule book
That the pine tar can only be a certain height,
And now they're trying to get rid of the bat,
And Gaylord Perry was out there,
He's gonna get fined,
He's in a tug-of-war with the umpire.

Dick Howser is furious.
They're holding George Brett out there,
Three men are holding him.
He is called out,
And the Yankees win the game four to three,
But it is one of the most unbelievable endings
I have ever seen.

> July 24, 1983 (The Pine Tar Game)
> Kansas City at New York
> Rich Gossage pitching to George Brett
> Ninth inning, one base runner, two outs
> Yankees lead 4–3
> (Brett's home run was later reinstated by
> the commissioner of baseball)

I Really Should Be
Going Home

It's very chilly.
As a matter—
I'm telling you,
I've been freezing.
My hands are cold.
I have low blood pressure anyway.
And arthritis.
I really should be going home.

July 24, 1983 (The Pine Tar Game)
Kansas City at New York
Mike Armstrong pitching to Rick Cerone
Seventh inning, bases empty, two outs
Yankees lead 4–3

Haiku

Ice, I can't stand it.
I cannot stand anything
Cold on my body.

May 31, 1991
Milwaukee at New York
Julio Machado pitching to Hensley Meulens
Eighth inning, no outs, bases empty
Score tied 2–2

Joe R.

Anyway . . .
Joe Rossomando
He was a good ballplayer.
I mean,
He looked a lot like Joe DiMaggio.
I'm tellin' ya,
He had a terrible collision at home plate.
In the minor leagues
And almost,
Almost swallowed his tongue
If it hadn't been
Uh,
For the trainer,
Came out,
Put a piece of wood in there.
Or something there.
Ohhh,
I couldn't look,
But he was an excellent player.
But anyway . . .
He's still coaching at Yale.
Just as old as I am.
He stays in great shape.
With his wife Marylou
And his daughter,
Mary Beth,
Who has graduated from Yale,
And has gone back

To take her master's there.
That's enough.

August 19, 1991, WPIX-TV
Kansas City at New York
Mike Boddicker pitching to Matt Nokes
Eighth inning, one out, one base runner
Score tied 2–2
Final: Yankees 6, Royals 2

Poem for Jesse

HEYYYYYYYYY!
THAT'S IT!
HOLY COW!
HE DID IT!
HOLY COW!
LOOK AT JESSE BARFIELD!
I WANNA TELL YOU!
HO HO HO HO!
WHOOOOOOOOOOOOOOAH!
YOU GOT IT, MURCER!
My heart.
My heart won't take it anymore.
I'm tellin' ya,
HOLY COW!
I MEAN,
THAT IS AN UNBELIEVABLE FINISH!
Are we on the air?
We're on the air?
We're on the?
Hooooooooooooooah.
WOW!
THIS YANKEE CLUB IS SOMETHING!
I TELL YA!
ATTA BOY, JESSE!

> May 31, 1991
> Milwaukee at New York
> Chuck Crim pitching to Jesse Barfield
> (Game-winning home run)
> Ninth inning, two outs, bases empty
> Yankees win 3–2

Squirrels

I.

In the backyard we got a lot of trees.
In our home I've watched them leap
From limb to limb.
Unbelievable.

II.

Did you ever get one in your attic?
They're not too cute
When they get in your attic.
I'll tell you that.

III.

I would not harm a squirrel.
I don't want to get those animal lovers . . .
I got them in my attic.
No, I got,
But I got a squirrel cage
And trapped them in the cage
Then took them out in the woods
Over by Yogi's house
And dropped them off.

June 7, 1991
Texas at New York
John Habyan pitching to Steve Buechele
Ninth inning, one out, bases empty
Tie score 4–4

Buns

He has powerful legs and cute buns,
That Henderson.
That was a great shot,
Going to second base there.
There's nothing wrong with that, White.
That's a popular expression.
High, and it's one and one.
His legs were churning.

May 10, 1987
New York at Minnesota
Charlie Hudson pitching to Al Newman
(Replay of stolen base)
Third inning, no outs, bases empty
Yankees lead 4–0

Legs

The legs are so important.
In golf they're very,
People don't realize
How important legs are in golf,
Or in baseball,
And football, definitely.
Track.
O, in track.
All-important.
Jumping.
Soccer.
Is there anything, what?
Is there anything where the legs
Are not the most important?

May 28, 1991
Boston at New York
Roger Clemens pitching to Jesse Barfield
Seventh inning, one out, bases empty
Red Sox lead 6—1

Rocket Love

Mmmmmmmm.
That's a lotta man there.
Got under it.
High pop-up.

May 28, 1991
Boston at New York
Roger Clemens pitching to Mel Hall
Sixth inning, two outs, one base runner
(Discussing Roger Clemens)
Red Sox lead 6–1

The Locked Door

We mention Buck Showalter.
He and I,
For twenty minutes,
Were trying to find a way
To get into the ballpark.

He was lucky.
He went down the tunnel.
But I couldn't go down there.
They said I didn't have the right credentials.
And I couldn't get in the door
That we got in tonight.

June 20, 1992
New York at Baltimore
Bob Milacki pitching to Mel Hall
First inning, one out, bases empty
No score

On Journalism

You gotta get down to the basic facts
You don't get, what?
Get the story if you want to be a good reporter.
And find out if it is true!
And then I hate it when I read it in the paper
Or TV comes out with a premature
FOUL BALL!
With a premature explanation.
Or whatever it is.

> June 22, 1991
> Minnesota at New York
> Wade Taylor pitching to Gene Larkin
> Sixth inning, two outs, bases empty
> Twins lead 2–0

Boxes

They have more fun with boxes
You know,
When during Christmas
Or any time
You go to buy the kids boxes.
That's what they play with.
You buy them beautiful toys.
They end up playing with the box.

July 27, 1991
California at New York
Greg Cadaret pitching to Dick Schofield
Fifth inning, no outs, bases empty
Yankees lead 4–2

60

Q

I used to hate that
When the trainer would
Come out.

Get that little piece of wood
And twirl part of your uh . . .
Q-tip.

Yeah, and roll it back and
You feel like your eyeball's gonna
Drop out.

August 6, 1979
Baltimore at New York
Dennis Martinez pitching to Willie Randolph
Third inning, bases empty, one out
Orioles lead 1–0

61

Oklahoma

Boy I tell ya.
My geography for that part of the country
Is terrible.
Probably because there's a lot of snakes
Out there.
And I don't want to care to know too much
About that part of the country.
Two balls
One strike.
They got snakes in Oklahoma?
No?
No kiddin?
Great!

May 25, 1991, WPIX-TV
New York at Baltimore
Seventh inning, one out, bases empty
John Habyan pitching to Mike Devereaux
Score tied 3–3
Final: Yankees 5, Orioles 4

F.Y.I.

A little high.
Two balls
No strikes.

Riverview Medical Center
Is down the Jersey shore.

Three balls
No strikes.

June 27, 1991, WPIX-TV
New York at Boston
Wade Taylor pitching to Tony Pena
Seventh inning, no outs, bases empty
Yankees lead 8–0
Final: Yankees 8, Red Sox 0

Concord

Everything is named Walden up there.
Yeah.
Great poet.
Great great poet.
Another one . . .
Uh.
I gotta think of the other one up the—
Another great poet that they . . .
It really is beautiful country.
I could very easily move up there.
I was thinking of Greenwich.
But I don't have enough money
To move up to Greenwich.
So I might move up to Concord.

September 20, 1991, WPIX-TV
New York at Boston
Scott Sanderson pitching to Scott Cooper
Seventh inning, two outs, bases empty
Red Sox lead 2–0
Final: Red Sox 2, Yankees 0

Paul Revere

I never knew that Paul Revere
Never made it to Concord.
He was ambushed right outside of Lexington.
And a fellow named Dawes picked up the—
It was almost like the pony express.
And he started out,
He didn't make it.
He got creamed
Somewhere between Lexington and Concord.
And then a fellow named Prescott
Finished it off.
And it's a strange thing.
But even in those days
You couldn't get a man to go nine.
Go the whole route.
You had to have a relief pitcher.
That is not a joke.
What was it?
It's not a good one.
Anyway . . .

September 20, 1991, WPIX-TV
New York at Boston
Scott Sanderson pitching to Tom Brunansky
Seventh inning, one out, bases empty
Red Sox lead 2–0
Final: Red Sox 2, Yankees 0

Mythkill

I'll say that a lot:
"Tonight,
We're going to Florida."
And they think
After the game
I fly to Florida.
And go down,
See the kids,
And come back the next day.

May 30, 1992
New York at Milwaukee
Scott Sanderson pitching to Greg Vaughn
Second inning, no outs, bases empty
Yankees lead 3–0

Bubbles

I.

There's a restaurant up in Westchester
Called the Roman Gardens.
Joe DiMaggio loves that place.
Italian food.
Anyway,
Nat Racine,
One of the owners,
Had invited me up there for lunch.
Right?
What is that, Little Dave?
What are you pointing at?
I was trying to tell a story here
And you interrupted me.

II.

This is lunch don't forget.
All the sudden I sit down.
And Nat's . . .
I always start a story too late.
That's three out.
You want a game over that's quick?
Get the Scooter in here!
At the end of seven and a half,
It's Toronto eleven and the Yankees one,
Now remember where I was, Seaver,
'Cause this is an unusual story.

III.

So . . .
Nat comes over and said,
Uhh.
And I didn't quite hear the whole sentence
That he said.
But he said,
He said,
Uhhhh.
All I heard was
"Don Perignon."
Right?

IV.

That's who I thought.
I had no idea.
And you know,
Lunch in the afternoon,
I figured . . .
So he poured me a glass.
And I'm not too much of a champagne drinker.
But I never did drink it.
Because every time I went to take a drink
The bubbles would hit me in the nose
And it felt so good
I just kept sitting there.
People must've thought I was nuts.

June 8, 1992
Toronto at New York
Lee Guetterman pitching to Jeff Kent
    Top of the seventh, two outs, bases empty
Bob MacDonald pitching to Kevin Maas
    Bottom of the seventh, no outs, bases empty
Blue Jays lead 11–1

California

It is weird out there.
California is kind of a weird state
Anyway . . .
I mean,
You go out there in the middle of the summer
And it's freezing.

June 9, 1992
Toronto at New York
Juan Guzman pitching to Charlie Hayes
Fifth inning, no outs, bases empty
Score tied 1–1

Greenwich Time

I.

Had a great time up in Greenwich.
It's a nice little town.
And you know,
You know what I like, Seaver,
About that town?
You can get two hours
On those meters in town.

II.

I got a ticket up in Windsor.
I parked for an hour and a half
And I had put money in it,
But they mark your tire
With the chalk mark.
I didn't know that.

III.

You're only allowed to stay an hour.
And I find I had to go to a county clerk
In a little wooden shack.
Pay 'em five dollars.

IV.

That's the only bad thing about Greenwich.
They don't have any parking areas.

You gotta wait for somebody
To pull out of a parking spot.

June 20, 1992
New York at Baltimore
Jeff Johnson pitching to Leo Gomez
Third inning, one out, bases empty
Yankees lead 6–4

Lake Effect

They had a warning out.
I was watching the television.
And they had that crawl underneath.
There was a—
No.
Not frostbite.
But they had waterspouts
Coming up in Lake . . .
Uh—
Lake Michigan.
What is it?
Lake Michigan?
It's not Lake Michigan.
Is it?

August 14, 1992
New York at Chicago
Scott Kamieniecki pitching to George Bell
Second inning, no outs, bases empty
No score

72

Colorado

They're having more snow
Out in Colorado.
Which is not in Montana.
But it is not far from Montana.

August 26, 1992
Milwaukee at New York
Sam Militello pitching to Darryl Hamilton
Third inning, one out, bases empty
Brewers lead 1–0

Zamboanga

When I was in the service
In the Philippines
I was in Zamboanga for a few days.
Fortunately,
I got out of there.
At the time
There was nothing there
But coconut trees.

August 28, 1992
New York at Minnesota
Scott Erickson pitching to Randy Velarde
Fourth inning, no outs, bases empty
Twins lead 1–0

74

This Planet Warm and Human

Mia.
Now Mia's been a very popular
Name in the newspapers lately,
Murcer.
I mean.

That took the headline.
Unbelievable!
Only in New York
Would it take the headlines away.
Yeah.

Unbelievable.
Terrible.
Terrible what's happening in that situation
And with all that going on down in Florida.
Boy.

They're still showing those pictures on TV
Of the damage down in Florida
By the way,
Are we going to Florida today,
Moore?
O that's in for a base hit!
Two runs will score!
No they won't.

August 30, 1992
New York at Minnesota
Sam Militello pitching to Brian Harper
Fourth inning, one out, two base runners
(Single scores one run)
Twins lead 1–0

Luck of the Irish

I can get this story in.
'Cause I just came back from Rochester.
I just started to talk about Joe Altobelli up in Rochester.
And Johnny Antonelli who lives in Rochester.
They have an Italian Open up there
For the benefit of the Boys and Girls Town of Italy.
And I mean,
The town is loaded with Italians.
Those beautiful names,
All ending in vowels that slip on . . .
O wonderful people!
Very . . .
Every once in a while,
An Irish,
Ryan or Something,
Would get in there.
Would just kind of break the melody
Of the Italian names.
And who do you think won the tournament?
There was like 200 Italians and about 6 Irishmen.
The Irishmen won.
LINED TO RIGHT,
AND DIVING . . .
IT'S BY HIM!
GROUND RULE DOUBLE!

September 15, 1992
Chicago at New York
Rich Monteleone pitching to Steve Sax
Eighth inning, one out, one base runner
Yankees lead 2–1

These Heaters

They're no good.
Because at my height
It goes over my head
And hits the guys in back of me.

I mean . . .

They were not built,
These heaters were not built
For normal human beings.
They were built for people like Seaver.

April 27, 1992
Texas at New York
Scott Sanderson pitching to Geno Petralli
Fourth inning, one out, one base runner
Yankees lead 3–1

Glasses

It seems like when we were playing, Jerry,
Only the outfielders wore them
And seldom maybe rarely the infielders wore them.
There's a strike to Howser.
And I think that it takes a lot of getting used to.
If you flip them down too quick, you're in trouble.
And if you flip them down too late, you're in trouble.
It's quite an art of flipping down those glasses.
The runners lead off first and second.
The pitch to Howser,
Swing and a foul tip, strike two.
Actually if the glasses are oiled up properly,
You just flip the tip of your cap.
You don't even have to touch the glasses and they'll fall
       down.
But if you have to flip two or three times,
And you're not following that ball,
When you flip them down,
As Jerry says, suddenly everything gets dark.

> May 21, 1967
> New York at Detroit
> Earl Wilson pitching to Dick Howser
> Sixth inning, two base runners, two out
> Tigers lead 7–0

My Nose

Now,
You wouldn't believe this!
When you were a kid
Did you ever have those fights,
You would get on,
On your buddy's back . . .
We called them elephant fights.
I don't know why.
We'd be elephant.
It'd be like Johnny on a Pony.
You get on
And you try to pull the other guy off
The other guy's back.
This was a game we played in Brooklyn.
And this kid swang around to get me,
Hit me with his elbow in the nose,
And I went to the teacher,
And said,
"I think my nose is broken."
She said,
"No, it's not."
And she wouldn't let me go home.
No.
No, it is NOT!
Not snot.
And she wouldn't let me go home.
And then it was too late to set the nose.
GOOD PLAY BY MAAS!

August 19, 1991
Kansas City at New York
Mike Boddicker pitching to Randy Velarde
Eighth inning, two outs, two base runners
Score tied 2–2
Final: Yankees 6, Royals 2

79

Dream Day

It turned out to be
One of the most beautiful days.
I had no idea
I was going to play golf today.
I didn't bring any shoes.
Or balls.
Or glove.
Or clothes.
But they . . .
They gave me a full complement.
And I was very embarrassed to take it.

May 26, 1992
New York at Minnesota
Pat Mahomes pitching to Mel Hall
First inning, one out, one base runner
Yankees lead 1-0

Symmetry

I wanna tell ya.
They replayed that game.
I got a chance to see it.
On MSG last night.
Man.
I mean,
Every game,
As you mentioned,
In Milwaukee
Was an exciting ball game.
They won two ball games
We should've won.
And we won two ball games
They should've won.
UNBELIEVABLE!

> May 26, 1992
> New York at Minnesota
> Pat Mahomes pitching to Mike Gallego
> First inning, no outs, bases empty
> No score

Wait a Minute

Wait a minute.
Wait a—
You can't call him "Scooter."
With me in the booth,
Seaver.
That name is . . .
That name is patented.

       May 30, 1992
       New York at Chicago
       Scott Sanderson pitching to Jim Gantner
       Third inning, one out, one base runner
       Yankees lead 3–0

Mattingly's Surprise

That's deep!
Down the left field line!
And gonna currrrrrrve.
HOLY COW!
A HOME RUN!
Ho ho ho.
RIGHT DOWN THE LINE!
LOOK:
Even Mattingly is surprised.

May 30, 1992
New York at Milwaukee
Chris Bosio pitching to Don Mattingly
Fourth inning, one out, two men on
(Double)
Yankees lead 8–0

Unwashed

I wouldn't eat anything now
After watching that bug walk on his hand.
I wouldn't shake hands with him either.

July 9, 1992
Seattle at New York
Greg Cadaret pitching to Tino Martinez
Eighth inning, no outs, one base runner
Yankees lead 7–5

Go Ahead, Seaver

You know,
Some kid wrote me a letter.
You and Murcer,
I know,
Every time Murcer says
I make oh for four and two errors.
Some guy wrote,
Which I haven't gotten yet,
He wrote it to Yankee Stadium,
But by the way,
You're doing the play-by-play, Seaver.
So go ahead.
I was gonna tell you something,
But I forgot what it was.
Go ahead.

July 1, 1991
Cleveland at New York
Lee Guetterman pitching to Chris James
Seventh inning, no outs, bases empty
Yankees lead 6–2

Thought for Seaver

It's funny
How certain words
In the English language
Could be very confusing.
You just said,
"They're idle this week."
Now you were an idol
Of all the kids at USC.
And it's spelled differently.
Idle and idol.
I just thought of that.

> September 7, 1991
> New York at Minnesota
> Pascual Perez pitching to Greg Gagne
> Fifth inning, two outs, bases empty
> Yankees lead 1–0

Instructions for the World

Watch this.
Forget about the script.
Don't read.
Don't read.
Ad-lib it.
And I had it upside down.

> May 30, 1992
> New York at Milwaukee
> Scott Sanderson pitching to Scott Fletcher
> Third inning, one out, bases empty
> Yankees lead 3–0

Reversal of Opinion

And he hits one in the hole
They're gonna have to hurry.
THEY'LL NEVER GET HIM!
They got him.
How do you like that.
Holy cow.
I changed my mind before he got there.
So that doesn't count as an error.

July 10, 1992
Seattle at New York
Dave Fleming pitching to Andy Stankiewicz
First inning, no outs, bases empty
Mariners lead 1–0

Observation

You know,
I was just thinking.
It's tough
To evaluate players
When you're out
On the golf course.

August 14, 1992
New York at Chicago
Alex Fernandez pitching to Matt Nokes
Seventh inning, two outs, bases empty
White Sox lead 2–0

To Blow a Story

I was talking with Sam McDowell.
You know Sam.
Great left-handed pitcher.
Very wild on and off the field.
Now he has settled down.
Does a great job.
Oh,
He's got his own clinic.
Anyway,
He told me that Bob Feller was popping off.
About how many pitches
He threw in one game.
Two hundred and sixty pitches.
McDowell said,
"Forget it!"
He threw two hundred NINETY pitches
In one inning.
Oh no . . .
Oh see . . .
I blew the . . .
I messed the . . .
Two hundred ninety pitches . . .
Not an inning.
I made a mistake.
I did.
I blew the story.
And it was a good story.

August 31, 1991, WPIX-TV
Toronto at New York
Greg Cadaret pitching to Roberto Alomar
Seventh inning, bases empty, no outs
Blue Jays lead 1–0
Final: Blue Jays 5, Yankees 0

To Finish a Story

One of the most embarrassing moments
In Mel Allen's life,
Not mine,
Was the day Mel and I
Were doing the game
At Cleveland's Municipal Stadium.
And the television booth
Was way on the third base side.
You talk about the game
While I finish this story.
And the radio was on the first base side.
And at the end of four and a half innings
We'd have to change positions.
The game started.
And McDowell was supposed to pitch.
And we said,
"McDowell's pitching!"
For seven innings
We had McDowell pitching.
Don't you go in on me,
Seaver.
This story's gonna be good by the end.
They got him!
Two outs.
I'm gonna finish this story.
Let me just finish this story.
In the seventh inning
Somebody calls from New York
Watching the game on PIX.
They said,
"That's not McDowell pitching.
"That's Kralick."
I laughed.
But Mel Allen wanted to throw
Our statistician out of the booth.

Poor Bill Kane.
He threw pencils at him,
Books at him.
Holy cow.

August 31, 1991, WPIX-TV
Toronto at New York
Greg Cadaret pitching to Joe Carter
Seventh inning, bases empty, two outs
(Carter grounds out to Espinoza)
Score: Blue Jays 1, Yankees 0
Final: Blue Jays 5, Yankees 0

Doom Balloon

Another balloon coming our way,
Seaver.
Must be a downdraft
Right here.
Pink balloon.
THAT SON OF A GUN'S COMING RIGHT—

August 14, 1992
New York at Chicago
Alex Fernandez pitching to Charlie Hayes
Third inning, two outs, bases empty
White Sox lead 1–0

Grew

Anyway . . .
Grew and I,
As I said,
We played 36
Holes of golf.
And if you ever
Saw Grew eat,
I mean,
He can eat.

August 7, 1992
Boston at New York
Scott Sanderson pitching to Scott Cooper
Seventh inning, two outs, bases empty
Yankees lead 4–0

Very Frustrated

I tell ya,
I tried that new McLean burger.
Very good.

Of course,
My cholesterol is very high.
Very high.

August 5, 1991
New York at Detroit
Jerry Don Gleaton pitching to Pat Kelly
Ninth inning, no outs, bases empty
Yankees lead 7–5

The Indelible Smell

What kind is it?
Ohhhhh!
Pepperoni!
Holy cow!
What happened?
Base hit!
A little disconcerting,
Smelling that pizza,
And trying
To do a ball game.

August 19, 1992
Oakland at New York
Mike Moore pitching to Charlie Hayes
Sixth inning, one out, bases empty
Yankees lead 4–1

Asylum

Got some chocolate-chip cookies here
Murcer.
So don't ask me any questions
For a batter or so.
All right?

June 17, 1992
New York at Boston
Roger Clemens pitching to Mel Hall
Sixth inning, two outs, bases empty
Red Sox lead 2–1

Possessions

Sanderson practicing the forkball.
Is that the new kid with him?
The new kid on the block?
Bob Wickman?
Yeah.
He wants the ball.
Sanderson won't give him the ball!
GIVE HIM THE BALL!
Fouled back and out of play.

August 26, 1992
Milwaukee at New York
Bill Wegman pitching to Randy Velarde
Second inning, one out, bases empty
Brewers lead 1–0

98

Surprise Attack

OH NOW!
SEAVER!
WITH THOSE STRONG FINGERS!
HE—
GAHHH!
HE JUST TAPS YOU ON THE BACK.
AND YOU'RE BLACK AND BLUE.
GAHHH!
COME ON!

September 4, 1992
Texas at New York
Matt Whiteside pitching to Mel Hall
Sixth inning, one out, one base runner
Yankees lead 6–3

Chess

I.

A lot of money in that chess.
I'll tell you that.
It's gotta be . . .
Can't be . . .
Not a good game for television.

II.

I'm not knocking it.
But it's not a spectator sport.

September 4, 1992
Texas at New York
Rich Monteleone pitching to Rafael Palmeiro
Seventh inning, no outs, bases empty
Yankees lead 6–3

Hall and Nokes

So second time around
Mel Hall and Matt Nokes
Solve Tapani's pitch.
Heh heh.
That's right.
John Moore's on the ball.
It does sound like a good rock group.
Hall and Nokes.
Oh?
Hall and Oates?
Oh yeah?
That's one I missed.
I'll have to go out
And buy some of their records tonight.

June 11, 1991
New York at Minnesota
Kevin Tapani pitching to Alvaro Espinoza
Fifth inning, two outs, two base runners
Twins lead 1–0

The Prince

I.

Last night I was watching TV.
I was watching Arsenio Hall.
And he had Prince on.
I wanna—
What a character he is!
Holy cow!

II.

Entertainer.
Singer.
And he can dance.
He's a little bitty guy.
He had a weird beard.
I tell ya it was—
I couldn't explain it.

III.

It was a real beard.
I mean,
You know how they do it now.
Some of them.
It doesn't come all the way
Up to the sideburns.
It starts,
Then it goes.
You gotta see it to believe it.

Sept. 10, 1991
New York at Baltimore
Eric Plunk pitching to Bill Ripken
Second inning, one out, one base runner
Yankees lead 2–1

Polonia's Hair

I.

Lookit.
I gotta tell my barber on Monday,
"Don't gimme a Polonia haircut."
Holy cow!

II.

That's the latest style.
It's just like
When new styles come out for women.
They wear it no matter how weird it looks.
They'll wear it 'cause it's a new style.

III.

Gonna get the women mad at me.
I'll think of something.
What?
I got another half minute
To think of something
To get out of this.

August 22, 1992
California at New York
Melido Perez pitching to Luis Sojo
Sixth inning, two outs, one base runner
Yankees lead 2–0

Mere Anarchy Is Loosed
upon the World

I tell ya.
Before long,
Football starts.
This weekend
In seriousness.
And pretty soon
It'll be hockey
And then basketball.
And then baseball
Will still
Be going on.
And it'll be
Very confusing,
Very confusing.

August 31, 1991, WPIX-TV
Toronto at New York
Eighth inning, bases empty, one out
Mike Timlin pitching to Pat Sheridan
Blue Jays lead 2–0
Final: Blue Jays 5, Yankees 0

Apodosis

Fly ball right field
It's gonna drop in.
No it's not gonna drop in.
Happy 46th wedding anniversary
Thomas and Mary Anne Clearwater.
That's it.
The last three, six, nine, twelve Yankees
Went down in order.
So that's it.
The game is over.

June 4, 1991
Toronto at New York
Tom Henke pitching to Pat Kelly
Ninth inning, two outs, bases empty
Blue Jays win 5–3

About the Author

Philip Francis Rizzuto (the Scooter) was born and raised in Brooklyn, New York. He played shortstop for the New York Yankees from 1941 until 1956. He retired a well-loved New York Yankee legend, with a lifetime batting average of .273. During his career he appeared in nine World Series, and won the American League's Most Valuable Player Award in 1950. In the early 1960s, still dedicated to the pinstripes, Rizzuto began broadcasting Yankee games for radio and television. His patented "Holy cow!" has a place in baseball history. Today, Phil Rizzuto still broadcasts Yankee games for WPIX-TV in New York. He has four children, Patricia Anne, Cynthia Anne, Penny Anne, and Philip (Scooter) Jr.; and lives in New Jersey with his wife Cora Anne.

About the Editors

In 1988 Hart Seely and Tom Peyer co-authored *Ronald Reagan's Contradictionary of the American Language.* Since then, their satire has appeared in *National Lampoon, The Village Voice, The New York Times, Harpers Magazine,* and on National Public Radio. Hart Seely, a reporter for the *Syracuse Herald-Journal* newspaper, lives in Manlius, NY, with his wife and two sons. Tom Peyer edits comic books with titles like *Animal Man, Doom Patrol,* and *Kid Eternity* for Vertigo/DC Comics. He has written a popular comic book biography of Mickey Mantle and drawn hundreds of editorial cartoons for the *Syracuse New Times.* He lives in New York with his wife.